THE PHOTOGRAPHS OF

ABRAHAM LINCOLN

FREDERICK HILL MESERVE

CARL SANDBURG

HARCOURT, BRACE AND COMPANY

NEW YORK

MGE

52009
920
L736m2

A WARTIME BOOK

*This complete edition is produced in full
compliance with the government's regu-
lations for conserving paper and other
essential materials.*

PRINTED IN THE UNITED STATES OF AMERICA

THE FACE OF LINCOLN

by CARL SANDBURG

Artists and sculptors, many painters and illustrators, common people of whom the Lord made many, have spoken of the fascination and the profound involvements to be seen in the face and physical form of Abraham Lincoln. The exterior man moved with some of the mystery of the interior man. Among contemporaries of Lincoln impressed by this memorable exterior was Gustave Koerner of Belleville, Illinois, who in March of 1861 noted the White House occupant as "neglected and unkempt," adding: "Something about the man, the face, is unfathomable." Having likeness to this was the comment in the same month from Henry Laurens Dawes, an able Congressman from Massachusetts, who said early in the Administration: "There is something in his face which I cannot understand. He is great. We can safely trust the Union to him," and years later: "I could never quite fathom his thoughts but it grew upon me that he was wiser than the men around him. He never altogether lost to me the look with which he met the curious and, for the moment, not very kind gaze of the House of Representatives on that first morning after what they deemed a pusillanimous creep into Washington. It was a weary look of one struggling to be cheerful under a burden of trouble." To Dawes and others the face of Lincoln indexed a cyclopedia of anxieties.

Many who came away from seeing Lincoln carried a dominant and lasting impression of him as a sober and sad man, his lapses into wit or humor fading again into the austere or the abstracted. John W. Widney of Piqua, Ohio, a sergeant wounded at the Wilderness, starting a furlough home for complete recovery before return to duty, saw Lincoln on the White House walk from the War Office, "dressed in black, with frock coat, stovepipe hat, walking slowly, shoulders bent forward, hands folded behind his back." He reminded Sergeant Widney of a Piqua man, "Old Mr. Orputt, an old time shoemaker, who lived in Park Avenue, an old time member of the Greene Street Church who always came to church in the same style clothes and wore a stovepipe hat." Lincoln asked the Sergeant, "What State and regiment?" Widney answered, and Lincoln, with a "God bless you and I hope you will get home safe," passed into the White House while Widney stood gazing and feeling a "burden of sorrow" on the shoulders under the stovepipe hat. Widney was a churchman who favored his

I

Bible and said that no other words fitted the moment for him like those of (to use his words) an old prophet: "O Jerusalem, Jerusalem, how often would I have gathered thee beneath my wings, as a hen gathers her chicks, but ye would not." So he quoted the passage.

The eminent comic David R. Locke of the *Toledo Blade*, who wrote under the pen name of Petroleum Vesuvius Nasby, like his fellow Buckeye from Piqua, on meeting and greeting Lincoln in a hotel room in Quincy, Illinois, during the debate with Douglas in 1858, also found a completely unconventional American to look at. Locke wrote: "I obtained an interview after the crowd had departed. He sat in the room with his boots off, to relieve his very large feet from the pain occasioned by continuous standing; or, to put it in his own words: 'I like to give my feet a chance to breathe.' He had removed his coat and vest, dropped one suspender from his shoulder, taken off his necktie and collar, and he sat tilted back in one chair with his feet upon another in perfect ease. He seemed to dislike clothing, and in privacy wore as little of it as he could."

They talked long and David R. Locke recorded his impression: "I never saw a more thoughtful face. I never saw a more dignified face. I never saw so sad a face."

Of like graphic solemnity was the little sketch by Francis Grierson of Lincoln beginning the speech at Alton, Illinois, in the debate with Douglas: "He rose from his seat, stretched his long, bony limbs upward as if to get them into working order and stood like some solitary pine on a lonely summit."

Mayor Henry Sanderson of Galesburg, Illinois, during the debate there helped with towels and warm water for Lincoln to take a bath; he saw Lincoln stripped, the lean, hard organization of muscles that sheathed the bony framework; and Sanderson told men about it afterward, with a quiet lighting of his face—"The strongest man I ever looked at."

One of the meanest, though cleverest, instances of funmaking at the expense of Lincoln's looks and ways was in a little mock biography in paper covers issued during the 1864 campaign: "Mr. Lincoln stands six feet twelve in his socks, which he changes once every ten days. His anatomy is composed mostly of bones, and when walking he resembles the offspring of a happy marriage between a derrick and a windmill. When speaking he reminds one of the old signal-telegraph that used to stand on Staten Island. His head is shaped something like a rutabago, and his complexion is that of a Saratoga trunk. His hands and feet are plenty large enough, and in society he has the air of having too many of them. The glove-makers have not yet had time to construct gloves that will fit him. In his habits he is by no means foppish, though he brushes his hair sometimes, and is said to wash. He swears fluently. A strict temperance man himself, he does not object to another man's being pretty drunk, especially when he is about to make a bargain with him. He is fond of fried liver and onions, and is a member of the church. He can hardly be called handsome, though he is certainly much better looking since he had the small-pox."

A vastly different impression of the personal presence of Lincoln is delivered by Noah Brooks writing for the *Chicago Tribune* of Lincoln's appearance before his Cooper Union audience in New York: "The tones, the gestures, the kindling eye, and the mirth-provoking look defy the reporter's skill. The vast assemblage frequently rang with cheers and shouts of applause. No man ever before made such an impression on his first appeal to a New York audience."

William H. Herndon, for sixteen years sharing the same office as junior law partner of Lincoln, noted of Lincoln's general structure "The whole man, body and mind, worked slowly, as if it needed oiling." And the face of Lincoln. When lights sprang into the gray eyes and fires of emotion flooded out over the scarred fissures, then "Sometimes it appeared as if Lincoln's soul was fresh from its creator."

One definite habit of Lincoln was to speak as though he was not so well-favored as to looks, more especially as to his face. On repeated occasions he remarked to some woman or to an audience, "In the matter of looks I have the advantage," meaning they had to look at him while he couldn't see himself. To an Illinois crowd in 1858 he said: "Nobody has ever expected me to be President. In my poor lean, lank face nobody has ever seen that any cabbages were sprouting out." Dropping in at a meeting of Republican editors in Decatur one time, he said he was a sort of interloper, and told of a woman on horseback meeting a man riding a horse on a narrow trail or pass. The woman stopped her horse, looked the man over, and broke out, "Well, for the land's sake, you are the homeliest man I ever saw!" The man replied, "Yes ma'am, but I can't help that," and the woman again, "No, I suppose not, but you might stay at home."

In a little autobiography written on request of a friend during the campaign of 1860 Lincoln sketched himself: "If any personal description of me is thought desirable, I am in height six feet four inches, nearly; lean in flesh, weighing, on an average, one hundred and eighty pounds; dark complexion, with coarse black hair and gray eyes."

In Dayton, Ohio, he sat for a daguerreotype, and a young man came in and began painting a portrait of him. "Keep on," he told the artist. "You may make a good one, but never a pretty one." Once, before posing for a photographer he stepped into a barbershop, saying, "I'd better get my hair slicked up." Then, sitting before the camera, he ran his fingers through his hair, caught himself, and said, "Guess I've made a bird's nest of it again."

Once when Lincoln's wife came to see him in his office, he was puzzled about the business in hand, and as his face took on an absent look Mrs. Lincoln said, "Mr. Lincoln, you look like you were having your picture taken."

He had a face he could manipulate, with take-off and put-on of look and tone, shadings in a gamut of the comedy of life. He was a practiced actor and an individual artist in the use of his face, when the going was good, and the time and company proper. He had grown up in a society where the theater and professional dramatic entertainments were scarce, and in the idle evenings and on rainy days people had to create art by themselves. The amateur entertainer was encouraged. It was an experienced comedian's face of which a biographer of Lincoln said in 1860: "His features are not handsome, but extremely mobile; his mouth particularly so. He has the faculty of contorting that feature to provoke uproarious merriment. Good humor gleams in his eye and lurks in the corner of his mouth." Thus he looked—in action.

Lincoln had often sat before a camera while a photographer stood with watch in hand counting the seconds till the "sitter" would be told "All right, it's over." In front of the sitter was the black box with the negative plate taking a sun print of his face, while behind him was an iron rack that his head fitted against while he kept his face muscles quiet, or stiff, till enough minutes had been counted off. Later, when proofs were brought to him, Lincoln left it to others to pick out the ones for final prints. Also it was others who urged him to have his pictures taken.

In his book of *Joe Miller's Jests* was an anecdote of two Frenchmen who were going to fight a duel. And one had stared long at the face of his enemy and said, "I can't fight with you," apologized, begged a thousand pardons, and explained, "If we fight I shall kill you and then I will remain the ugliest fellow in the kingdom."

It was a story much like Lincoln's of his meeting a man who handed him a pistol, saying, "I promised long ago that if I ever met a man uglier than myself I would hand him this pistol and tell him to shoot me." And Lincoln had answered, after searching the fellow's face, "Well, if I am uglier than you are, for God's sake, go ahead and shoot." Thus the story was told.

Perhaps such stories flitted through his mind as he sat one day before a mirror in a room in the Borland Block in Chicago, with plaster over all of his face except the eyes. He was breathing through quills stuck through the plaster and into his nose. It was part of what he had to go through for the sculptor Leonard W. Volk, who wanted to make a bust of him. Every morning after breakfast for several days he went to Volk's studio till a life mask, a fine documentation of the Lincoln face in repose, was completed. Later Volk came to Springfield to make casts of President-elect Lincoln's hands, and as the finished likeness emerged from the clay, Lincoln said, "There's the animal himself."

The photographer Hesler came one day from Chicago. Politicians there were saying Lincoln seemed to be in "rough everyday rig" in all his pictures. Lincoln had written he would be "dressed up" if Hesler came to Springfield. And Hesler made four negatives of Lincoln in a stiff-bosomed pleated shirt with pearl buttons. The glister of the shirt was the equal of any in a Douglas photograph, which was what the politicians were demanding.

One odd piece of American history and folklore reports a girl twelve years old in Westfield, New York, writing to Lincoln that he would look better if he wore whiskers. She gave her name, age, address, and asked Lincoln if he had no time to answer her letter to allow his little girl to reply for him. The country heard through the press of Lincoln en route to Washington finishing a speech at Westfield with asking Grace Bedell to come forward. Then he shook hands with her, kissed her, touched his beard, and said, "You see, I let these whiskers grow for you, Grace."

John G. Nicolay, the faithful and scrupulous private secretary, set forth as well-known peculiarities of Lincoln's form and features: "Large head, with high crown of skull; thick, bushy hair; large and deep eye-caverns; heavy eyebrows; a large nose; large ears; large mouth, thin upper and somewhat thick under lip; very high and prominent cheekbones; cheeks thin and sunken; strongly developed jawbones; chin slightly upturned; a thin but sinewy neck, rather long; long arms; large hands; chest thin and narrow as compared with his great height; legs of more than proportionate length, and large feet."

What some observers took to be a loose, lank, awkward physical frame operated to hide from them the fact that Lincoln was all his life an athlete, sometimes slow to get going but when in stride having panther quality. When President he more than once picked up an ax with his right hand and held it full horizontal at arm's length, doing this with a half-amused pride. "He was a spare, bony, lean, and muscular man, which gave him great and untiring tenacity of endurance," wrote Thomas D. Jones, a Cincinnati sculptor who in December, 1860, made a bust of Lincoln. He wrote of hearing Lincoln say, "All I had to do was to extend one hand to a man's shoulder, and with weight of body and strength of arms give him a trip that generally sent him sprawling on the ground, which would so astonish him as to give him a quietus."

One of the keenest and most important studies of the Lincoln face is by the same Nicolay, who traveled from Springfield to Washington with Lincoln and stayed to the end. "The question of looks depended in Lincoln's case very much upon his moods," wrote Nicolay. "The large framework of his features was greatly modified by the emotions which controlled them. The most delicate touch of the painter often wholly changes the expression of a portrait; his inability to find that one needed master touch causes the ever-recurring wreck of an artist's fondest hopes. In a countenance of strong lines and rugged masses like Lincoln's, the lift of an eyebrow, the curve of a lip, the flash of an eye, the movements of prominent muscles created a much wider facial play than in rounded immobile countenances. Lincoln's features were the despair of every artist who undertook his portrait. The writer saw nearly a dozen, one after another, soon after the first nomination to the presidency, attempt the task. They put into their pictures the large rugged features, and strong prominent lines; they made measurements to obtain exact proportions; they 'petrified' some single look, but the picture remained hard and cold. Even before these paintings were finished it was plain to see that they were unsatisfactory to the artists themselves, and much more so to the intimate friends of the man; this was not he who smiled, spoke, laughed, charmed. The picture was to the man as the grain of sand to the mountain, as the dead to the living. Graphic art was powerless before a face that moved through a thousand delicate gradations of line and contour, light and shade, sparkle of the eye and curve of the lip, in the long gamut of expression from grave to gay, and back again from the rollicking jollity of laughter to that serious, faraway look that with prophetic intuitions beheld the awful panorama of war, and heard the cry of oppression and suffering. There are many pictures of Lincoln; there is no portrait of him."

Of the penetrating eyes of Lincoln, John Hay had once commented when a certain overdressed fraud appeared: "He looked through the man to the buttons on the back of his coat."

Noah Brooks, somewhat scholar and dreamer, a failure as merchant in Illinois and farmer in Kansas, correspondent of the *Sacramento Union* writing under the pen name of "Castine" newsletters widely reprinted on the West coast, often had close touch with Lincoln, and wrote of one phase: "He was cordial and affable, and his simple-hearted manners made a strong impression upon those who saw him for the first time. I have known impressionable women, touched by his sad face and his gentle bearing, to go away in tears. Once I found him sitting in his chair so collapsed and weary that he did not look up or speak when I addressed him. He put out his hand, mechanically, as if to shake hands, when I told him I had come at his bidding. It was several minutes before he was roused enough to say that he 'had had a hard day.'"

An associate lawyer, Henry Clay Whitney, heard Lincoln quote lines: "Mortal man, with face of clay, Here tomorrow, gone today."

Edwin McMasters Stanton, a high-priced lawyer and a good one, who a few years later was appointed by Lincoln to be Secretary of War, in 1859 was trying an important patent case in Cincinnati with Lincoln as a minor associate attorney. When Stanton's eyes lighted on Lincoln at the Burnett House in Cincinnati, wearing heavy boots, loose clothes, farmer-looking, he framed his astonishment in the question "Where did that long-armed baboon come from?" And he later described Lincoln as wearing a linen duster with splotches like "a dirty map of the continent," and was quoted as saying he wouldn't associate with "such a damned, gawky, long-armed ape as that."

Round the world to the readers of that molder and register of British upper-class opinion, the London *Times*, had gone William Howard Russell's plain-spoken account: "A person who met Mr. Lincoln in the street would not take him to be what—according to the usages of European society—is called a 'gentleman'; and, indeed, since I came to the United States, I have heard more disparaging allusions made by Americans to him on that account than I could have expected among simple republicans, where all should be equals; but, at the same time, it would not be possible for the most indifferent observer to pass him in the street without notice." Russell would read character by a mouth. "One would say that, although the mouth was made to enjoy a joke, it could also utter the severest sentence which the head could dictate, but that Mr. Lincoln would be ever more willing to temper justice with mercy, and to enjoy what he considers the amenities of life, than to take a harsh view of men's nature and the world, and to estimate things in an ascetic or puritan spirit."

One sketch of Lincoln by Russell ran: "He was dressed in an ill-fitting, wrinkled suit of black, which put one in mind of an undertaker's uniform at a funeral; round his neck a rope of black silk was knotted in a large bulb, with flying ends projecting beyond the collar of his coat; his turned-down shirt-collar disclosed a sinewy muscular yellow neck, and above that, nestling in a great black mass of hair, bristling and compact like a ruff of mourning pine, rose the strange quaint face and head, covered with its thatch of wild republican hair, of President Lincoln. The impression produced by the size of his extremities, and by his flapping and wide projecting ears, may be removed by the appearance of kindliness, sagacity, and the awkward bonhommie of his face; the mouth is absolutely prodigious; the lips, straggling and extending almost from one line of black beard to the other, are only kept in order by two deep furrows from the nostril to the chin; the nose itself—a prominent organ—stands out from the face, with an inquiring, anxious air, as though it were sniffing for some good thing in the wind; the eyes dark, full, and deeply set, are penetrating, but full of an expression which almost amounts to tenderness; and above them projects the shaggy brow, running into the small hard frontal space, the development of which can scarcely be estimated accurately, owing to the irregular flocks of thick hair carelessly brushed across it."

Thus one English journalist. Still another Londoner, who wrote pieces for *Once a Week*, achieved a different portrait: "This is the great leader of the Republican party—Abolitionist—terror of the Democrats—an honest old lawyer, with face half Roman, half Indian, wasted by climate, scarred by a life's struggle."

"A Hoosier Michael Angelo," that was Lincoln, outside and inside, to the poet Walt Whitman. He wrote in a diary: "Called at the President's house on John Hay. Saw Mr. Lincoln standing, talking with a gentleman, apparently a dear friend. His face and manner have an expression inexpressibly sweet—one hand on his friend's shoulder, the other holding his hand. I love the President personally."

Of the President and his party driving from the White House to Soldiers' Home Whitman noted: "I saw very plainly the President's dark brown face, with the deep cut lines, the eyes . . . always to me with a deep latent sadness in the expression. . . . They pass'd me once very close, and I saw the President in the face fully, as they were moving slow, and his look, though abstracted, happen'd to be directed steadily in my eye. I noticed well the expression I have alluded to. None of the artists have caught the deep, though subtle and indirect expression of this man's face. They have only caught the surface. There is something else there. One of the great portrait painters of two or three centuries ago is needed."

The Alton Railroad conductor Gilbert Finch said people could get near Lincoln in a sort of neighborly way, as though they had always known him. "But there was something tremendous between you and him all the time," said Finch. "I have eaten with Lincoln many times at the railroad eating-houses, and you get very neighborly if you eat together in railroad restaurants. Everybody tried to get as near Lincoln as possible when he was eating, because he was such good company. But we couldn't exactly make him out. Sometimes I would see what looked like dreadful loneliness in his look, and I used to wonder what he was thinking about. Whatever it was he was thinking alone. It wasn't a solemn look, like Stephen A. Douglas sometimes had. Douglas sometimes made me think of an owl; he stared at you with dark eyes in a way that almost frightened you.

"Lincoln never frightened anybody," said the Alton conductor. "No one was afraid of him. But something about him made plain folks feel toward him a good deal as a child feels toward his father."

There came to be registered on Lincoln's face some of the poetry of his having said of "Popular Sovereignty" that it was "nothing but a living, creeping lie" and of one Douglas argument that it got down as thin as "soup made by boiling the shadow of a pigeon that had starved to death."

Picking up a trick compliment from Douglas, he smiled it into thin air with the comment "Not being accustomed to flattery, it came the sweeter to me."

Henry Villard, a *New York Herald* correspondent, late in 1860 wrote: "Mr. Lincoln's face is a study—especially when lighted up. I have never seen a picture of him that does anything like justice to the original. He is a much better-looking man than any of the pictures represent." Villard compared Lincoln's looks to those of two respectable Easterners, and gave Lincoln the best of it. "I do not understand why Mr. Lincoln is represented as being so prodigiously ugly. Put him alongside Mr. Charles O'Connor and Mr. James W. Gerard—both of which eminent gentlemen have ridiculed so much his supposed ugliness—and if he would not appear 'as Adonis to a satyr,' he would at all events be set down as the finest-looking man of the trio."

To the White House often had come the master photographer Mathew B. Brady. Since February of 1860, at the time of the Cooper Union speech, Brady had in the autumn of 1864 photographed Lincoln more than thirty times. From his profitable portrait gallery on Broadway and Tenth, New York, Brady had come to the war with his camera. Out in the camps, on the march, and on battlefields Brady and his assistants made both single and stereoscopic wet-plate exposures, and were achieving a camera record comprising thousands of convincing likenesses of scenes and people. It was said Brady urged Lincoln to have him co-operate with the Government and make as complete as possible a camera chronicle of the war for the War Department archives, and that Lincoln had refused to support the plan. As next best, Lincoln wrote and signed a heavy card with the large scrawl "Pass Brady," which took Brady nearly anywhere he cared to go.

Collections of cartes de visite (French for visiting card, and with your name you left your face), photographs of fine clarity and definition of line, mounted on small cards usually 2½" x 4" in size, were in many thousands of homes. Brady and Gardner photographs of Lincoln were often on show there. Frequently the illustrated weeklies *Harper's* and *Leslie's*, and occasionally the daily newspapers, published large drawings from photographs, so that Lincoln's face and figure had become familiar to the literate population, to those who read, and of course to some who enjoyed pictures though they read not.

Montgomery Blair told Carpenter that one of the early pictures of Lincoln, "a hideous painting," had given an unfavorable impression of the President's looks. Carpenter replied: "My friend, Brady the photographer, insisted that his photograph of Mr. Lincoln, taken the morning of the day he made his Cooper Union speech . . . was the means of his election.

That it helped largely to this end I do not doubt. The effect of such influences, though silent, is powerful."

A Connecticut painter's portrait of Lincoln, done for Secretary Welles, hung temporarily on the wall of Lincoln's office. Welles, turning toward it one afternoon, said it was a successful likeness. From Lincoln came a hesitant "Yes," noted Carpenter, and a story of a Western man who had himself painted secretly and gave his wife the picture for a birthday present. "Horridly like," she pronounced it. "And that," said Lincoln, "seems to me a just criticism of *this!*"

James R. Gilmore, author and journalist, noted: "A smile positively transfigured his whole face, making his plain features actually good-looking, so that I could agree with Caroline M. Kirkland, who not long before had told me that he was the handsomest man she had ever seen." A living characteristic of Lincoln was his facial mobility. When it was not there he was "gaunt, woe-begone," as Sergeant Stradling, a Quaker youth who called on Lincoln at the White House, had noticed. "A puzzled shadow settled on his features and his eyes had an inexpressible sadness in them, with a faraway look," said the painter Thomas Hicks. There was "a lack of apparent force" as Henry Adams saw him handshaking at a reception.

The faraway look was in the impression set down by Charles Francis Adams, Jr.: "The only remark Lincoln made to me was—'A son of Charles Francis Adams? I am glad to see you, sir'; but at the same time I saw a look of interest. Lincoln's face is a good one, and he has proved his skill as a debater; but, if I could judge from a passing glance at a moment when the man was obviously embarrassed, I should say that his eye never belongs to a man great in action; it is neither the quick sharp eye of a man of sudden and penetrating nature, nor the slow firm eye of one of decided will; but it is a mild, dreamy, meditative eye which one would scarcely expect to see in a successful chief magistrate in these days of the republic. *Mais nous verrons.*"

At times the President near the White House, or at some of the government departments, when spoken to passed on with abstracted face, not speaking in return, and they knew his mind was far away. The mobility of face might come quickly. One spoke of "his summer lightning smile," another of his face as "an ever-varying mirror."

The mobility of the Lincoln face does baffle description. The range of his facial expression is beyond registration in words. This goes straight back to the wide range of his personality. Besides a natural melancholy in his very bones—and an intelligence sensitively aware of human tragedy and weighed down by it—he had the gift of laughter alive to either earthy and Rabelaisian horseplay or fine, thin ironics that you had to hear twice to be sure they were there. Over and again men told of how he was sunk in abstractions, solemnity, melancholy, sobriety, and then something happened to wake the lights in him and his whole face began not merely to change but to go through series of swift changes in accompaniment to what he or others were saying.

In September of 1848, stumping New England for the national Whig ticket, a young Whig, George H. Monroe, and others, called at the Tremont House in Boston to take Lincoln to Dedham for a day speech. "He was as sober a man in point of expression as I ever saw," said Monroe. "In the cars he scarcely said a word to one of us. He seemed uneasy. . . . We took him to one of the most elegant houses in the town of Dedham, and here he seemed still less at home. The thing began to look rather blue for us. When we went over to the hall it was not much better. It was a small hall and only about half full; for Mr. Lincoln had not spoken in Boston yet, and there was nothing in his name particularly to attract. But at last he arose to speak, and almost instantly there was a change. His indifferent manner vanished as soon as he opened his mouth. He went right to work. He wore a black alpaca sack, and he turned up the sleeves of this, and then the cuffs of his shirt. Next he loosened his necktie, and soon after he took it off altogether. All the time he was gaining upon his audience. He soon had it as by a spell. I never saw men more delighted. His style was the most familiar and offhand possible. His eye had lighted up and changed the whole expression of his countenance."

Lincoln's transition from mood to mood impressed Andrew D. White, educator and a member of the New York State senate. White saw Lincoln in the White House "dressed in a rather dusty suit of black," resembling "some rural tourist who had blundered into the place." Lincoln entered the room and approached White's group. He seemed, to White, "less at home there than any other person present" as he "looked about for an instant as if in doubt where he should go." Others had seen and written of the same thing. And White's impression recorded itself: "As he came toward us in a sort of awkward, perfunctory way his face seemed to me one of the saddest I had ever seen, and when he had reached us he held out his hand to the first stranger, then to the second and so on all with the air of a melancholy automaton. But suddenly someone in the company said something which amused him and instantly there came in his face a most marvelous transformation. I have never seen anything like it in any other human being. His features were lighted, his eyes radiant, he responded to sundry remarks humorously, then dryly, and thenceforward was cordial and hearty. Taking my hand in his he shook it in the most friendly way, with a kindly word, and so passed cheerily on to the others till the ceremony was finished." It interested White to hear later from Robert Lincoln that "when any attempt was made to photograph his father or to paint his portrait, he relapsed into his melancholy mood."

Young Horace White of the *Chicago Tribune* saw Lincoln through the debates with Douglas and on through years in the White House—and White wrote with feeling and color of how Lincoln's sense of humor was fatefully intermeshed with the man's everyday behavior and democratic habits. "I have seen him a hundred times," noted White, "his lantern jaws and large mouth and solid nose firmly set, his sunken eyes looking at nothing yet not unexpressive, his wrinkled and retreating forehead cut off by a mass of tousled hair, with a shade of melancholy drawn like a veil over his whole face. Nothing more unlike this can be imagined than the same Lincoln when taking part in a conversation, or addressing an audience, or telling a story. The dull listless features dropped like a mask. The melancholy shadow disappeared in a twinkling. The eye began to sparkle, the mouth to smile, the whole countenance was wreathed in animation, so that a stranger would have said, 'Why, this man, so angular and somber a moment ago, is really handsome.'"

Isaac N. Arnold, whose humor, like that of Nicolay, seldom rose to the surface, quoted "What has made this joyous merry man so sad? What great sorrow lies at his heart?" The mingling of these extremes in Lincoln affected his loyal friend. "Mirthfulness and melancholy, hilarity and sadness, were strangely combined in him. His mirth was sometimes exuberant. It sparkled in jest, story and anecdote, while at the next moment, his peculiarly sad, pathetic, melancholy eyes would seem to wander far away, and one realized that he was a man 'familiar with sorrow and acquainted with grief.'"

On the day after Fredericksburg Isaac N. Arnold entered Lincoln's office to find the President reading the works of Artemus Ward. The staggering defeat, the rivers of blood gone, the topic of informed men everywhere, was not touched by the President. He asked Arnold to sit down and he would read Artemus Ward's description of a visit to the Shakers, a sect who had a communal form of life, believed in plain clothing for all occasions and fantastic moaning and holy rolling at their religious services. Ward wrote that one spring he got "swampt in the exterior of New York State, one dark and stormy night, when the winds Blue pityusly, and I was forced to tie up with the Shakers." He knocked at a door. "A solum female, looking sumwhat like a last year's beanpole stuck into a long meal bag, axed me was I athurst and did I hunger? to which I urbanely answered 'a few.'"

That Lincoln should wish to read this sort of nonsense while the ambulances were yet hauling thousands of wounded from the frozen mud flats of the Rappahannock River was amazing to Congressman Arnold. As he said afterward, he was "shocked." He inquired, "Mr. President, is it possible that with the whole land bowed in sorrow and covered with a pall in the presence of yesterday's fearful reverse, you can indulge in such levity?" Then, as Arnold said it happened, as he saw and heard, the President threw down the Artemus Ward book, tears streamed down his cheeks, his physical frame quivered as he burst forth, "Mr. Arnold, if I could not get momentary respite from the crushing burden I am constantly carrying, my heart would break!" And with that pent-up cry let out, it came over Arnold that the laughter of Lincoln at times was a mask.

Nathaniel Hawthorne wrote for the *Atlantic Monthly* an article on his visit to Washington and the White House. Part of Hawthorne's sketch of Lincoln the editor of the *Atlantic* deleted with the comment "Considered as the portrait of a living man it would not be wise or tasteful to print." Hawthorne wrote a footnote: "We are compelled to omit two or three pages, in which the author describes the interview, and gives his idea of the personal appearance and deportment of the President. The sketch appears to have been written in a benign spirit, and perhaps conveys a not inaccurate impression of its august subject; but it lacks *reverence*, and it pains us to see a gentleman of ripe age, and who has spent years under the corrective influence of foreign institutions, falling into the characteristic and most ominous fault of Young America." The deleted paragraphs which failed to reach the eyes of the readers of the *Atlantic* read as follows:

"By and by there was a little stir on the staircase and in the passageway, and in lounged a tall, loose-jointed figure, of an exaggerated Yankee port and demeanor, whom (as being about the homeliest man I ever saw, yet by no means repulsive or disagreeable) it was impossible not to recognize as Uncle Abe.

"Unquestionably, Western man though he be, and Kentuckian by birth, President Lincoln is the essential representative of all Yankees, and the veritable specimen, physically, of what the world seems determined to regard as our characteristic qualities. It is the strangest and yet the fittest thing in the jumble of human vicissitudes, that he, out of so many millions, unlooked for, unselected by any intelligible process that could be based upon his genuine qualities, unknown to those who chose him, and unsuspected of what endowments may adapt him for his tremendous responsibility, should have found the way open for him to fling his lank personality into the chair of state,—where, I presume, it was his first impulse to throw his legs on the council-table, and tell the Cabinet Ministers a story.

"There is no describing his lengthy awkwardness, nor the uncouthness of his movement; and yet it seemed as if I had been in the habit of seeing him daily, and had shaken hands with him a thousand times in some village street; so true was he to the aspect of the pattern American, though with a certain extravagance which, possibly, I exaggerated still further by the delighted eagerness with which I took it in. If put to guess his calling and livelihood, I should have taken him for a country school-master as soon as anything else.

"He was dressed in a rusty black frock coat and pantaloons, unbrushed, and worn so faithfully that the suit had adapted itself to the curves and angularities of his figure, and had grown to be an outer skin of the man. He had shabby slippers on his feet. His hair was black, still unmixed with gray, stiff, somewhat bushy, and had apparently been acquainted with neither brush nor comb that morning, after the disarrangement of the pillow; and as to a nightcap, Uncle Abe probably knows nothing of such effeminacies. His complexion is dark and sallow, betokening, I fear, an insalubrious atmosphere around the White House; he has thick black eyebrows and an impending brow; his nose is large, and the lines about his mouth are very strongly defined.

"The whole physiognomy is as coarse a one as you would meet anywhere in the length and breadth of the States; but, withal, it is redeemed, illuminated, softened, and brightened by a kindly though serious look out of his eyes, and an expression of homely sagacity, that seems weighted with rich results of village experience.

"A great deal of native sense; no bookish cultivation, no refinement; honest at heart, and thoroughly so, and yet, in some sort, sly,—at least, endowed with a sort of tact and wisdom that are akin to craft, and would impel him, I think, to take an antagonist in flank, rather than to make a bull-run at him right in front. But, on the whole, I like this sallow, queer, sagacious visage, with the homely human sympathies that warmed it; and, for my small share in the matter, would as lief have Uncle Abe for a ruler as any man whom it would have been practicable to put in his place."

Hawthorne of course did not know the Midwest or Kentucky with the firsthand acquaintance that he knew his New England people. The same would go for Colonel Theodore Lyman of General Meade's staff. In a letter to his wife one evening Lyman gave her his impression of what he believed he saw when he gazed at Lincoln then visiting the Army of the Potomac in early '65. An heir to an independent fortune, a Harvard graduate and a European traveler, a devotee of science who in his work under Agassiz had become a leading authority on the ophiurans (star-shaped and disklike relative of the sea urchin), now of nearly two years' loyal service in the field with Meade, Lyman wrote home a terse, frank appraisal of the President, a thumbnail portrait. It was meant for his wife to read. It was in confidence. It was what he would have answered her in their Brookline mansion if she over the breakfast coffee had asked him, "What was your impression of Lincoln as you saw him?" He wrote for her:

"The President is, I think, the ugliest man I ever put my eyes on; there is also an expression of plebeian vulgarity in his face that is offensive (you recognize the recounter of coarse stories). On the other hand, he has the look of sense and wonderful shrewdness, while the heavy eyelids give him a mark almost of genius. He strikes me, too, as a very honest and kindly man; and, with all his vulgarity, I see no trace of low passions in his face. On the whole, he is such a mixture of all sorts, as only America brings forth. He is as much like a highly intellectual and benevolent Satyr as anything I can think of. I never wish to see him again, but, as humanity runs, I am well content to have him at the head of affairs."

Grace Greenwood, the author, noted that the President, dressed in somber black, had white kid gloves giving "a rather ghastly effect on his large, bony hands." Talking with him, she found him easier to look at. "Before I heard his sweet-toned voice and saw his singularly sympathetic smile, Mr. Lincoln was certainly an awesome personage to me." She read his face as "furrowed and harrowed by infinite perplexities, while over all was a simple dignity more than sacerdotal—a peculiar, set-apart look, which I have never seen in any other man." This was her impression at a party where the Lincoln family met General and Mrs. Tom Thumb. Lincoln, as Miss Greenwood saw him, held Mrs. Thumb's hand "with special chariness, as though it were a robin's egg, and he were afraid of breaking it."

In the very angles and planes of the Lincoln face utterly grave, may be found suggestions of the mobility, humor, and riotous laughter that occasionally ran over these features. The three foremost humorists of his time were his affectionate friends, and they had in common their understanding of the questions "What is it all about? Shall we sometimes rather laugh than weep?"

Life so often took ridiculous hazards, and pomp and power shuffled with a limping dignity if looked at long enough, so implied the horselaugh philosophers praised by Lincoln. The fields of politics and war saw swindlers, pretenders, hypocrites, demagogues, charlatans, bootlickers, snivelers, shifters, incompetents. They held that democracy, the experiment of popular government, could never be anything else than a series of approximations, imperfections incessantly present or arriving. Democracy would be achieved only through humanity, its operations conducted by and through the members of the human family. Behind the exterior of mirth, under the jokery, seemed so often to be the quizzical thrusting: "What is man? Why does he behave as he does? Is it absurd that I, who am a man, should cut up and play such capers as you see me in?"

A famous European sculptor of a later generation exclaimed on seeing a photograph of Lincoln, "He is a new type!" From several other sources came the comment that he was a type foreshadowing democracy. The inventive Yankee, the Western frontiersman and pioneer, the Kentuckian of laughter and dreams, had found blend in one man who was the national head. In the "dreamy vastness" noted by the London *Spectator*, in the pith of the folk words "The thoughts of the man are too big for his mouth," was the feel of something vague that ran deep in American hearts, that hovered close to a vision for which men would fight, struggle, and die, a grand tough blurred chance that Lincoln might be leading them toward something greater than they could have believed might come true.

FREDERICK HILL MESERVE

by CARL SANDBURG

One unforgettable moment in the life and work of Frederick H. Meserve happened in Hoboken, New Jersey. He had talked about buying a collection of glass negatives the day before. And on this day he went to Hoboken to see what he had and how to pack and haul it home if he bought it. On the warehouse floor lay scores of glass negatives—broken. They had sort of spilled over. There were thousands more—who cared? Meserve saw on the floor one negative not broken. He picked it up and held it to the light. His eyes ranged over it. And he could hardly believe his eyes. What he saw was a camera record, an extraordinary photographic negative, a profile of the face and right shoulder of Abraham Lincoln, a composed, majestic Abraham Lincoln. What he saw was the camera record of the granitic Lincoln in February, 1864, facing the awful issues of that year of smoke, agony, and ballots.

Up to this time Meserve had been a patient and devoted collector of the known Lincoln photographs. Now he became a tireless zealot. There are collectors who are hobbyists, fans, faddists, enthusiasts, eccentrics, cranks, bugs. Meserve is the Zealot. When he closes his desk and leaves his business office to see that evening sun go down when day is done, he takes the subway home to a realm of the faces of the past where he immerses himself in photographs, ambrotypes, daguerreotypes, cartes de visite, and the lore thereof. Not quite half joking, he has been known to say, "I have lived a double life without being secret."

Like any millionaires who don't know from day to day how many millions they rate, Meserve can't tell us just how many antique photographs and old negatives he has: "Somewhere over two hundred thousand—at least that many." Thousands are in fireproof storage, and he hopes sometime to see them all classified and arranged with data and memoranda for permanent use and practical service. He believes the scope of his accumulations and the care he has given them have resulted in at least a few priceless photographs being saved from destruction or spoilage. Certainly that goes for a number of Civil War and Lincoln photographs.

In the field of the Lincoln photographs Meserve found his dominant special interest. Those who know his methods and his endless devotion in this field believe it is quite probable that certain Lincoln photographs would not have come to light but for Meserve. They would still be hiding in obscurity or lost for all time. The total of one hundred and twenty known Lincoln photographs might well be only a hundred and ten or a hundred or less had it not been for Meserve and his persistent researches and his intelligent use of his findings.

His interest in the Civil War and Lincoln may follow in part from his father, who fought in battle, prayed in dark hours, and wrote letters and articles to the home paper in support of Lincoln. From a personal record based on diary notes kept by William Neal Meserve, later written by him into a narrative titled "A Volunteer," he is seen in plenty of action. "In the summer of 1862," he wrote, "when it became evident to every patriot that the rebellion was a power and the country needed men I felt it my duty to enlist. President Lincoln had called for three hundred thousand more and he called me. I joined Captain Wm. S. King's company at Roxbury, Mass., July 28, 1862, and well remember with what hesitation I signed the roll well knowing that my signature implied three years of probable hard and dangerous service. Twice my resolution faltered; a few who declared they would enlist with me weakened also though one of them afterward came forward; my third attempt was a success and my name became the 41st on the list. Going home that night quite late, my father having retired, I called to him saying that I had enlisted; 'What, William?' and then presently he found breath to say that it was the worst day's work of my life as I couldn't in his opinion possibly stand a soldier's hardships."

Three times while serving till the war's end, Meserve saw President Lincoln. Of October 27, 1862, he wrote: "A rainy day, we lifted our chattels to our backs and turned southward. . . . Before leaving Pleasant Valley President Lincoln reviewed the army and occasioned unbounded enthusiasm as he rode along the lines. It was the only time I saw him in the field." That was under McClellan and the Army of the Potomac, a few weeks after the battle of Antietam. Of April 23, 1864, he wrote: "We headed for Washington, reaching and passing through which President Lincoln reviewed us from the balcony of Willard's Hotel." Of the late October and early November days just before Lincoln's re-election Meserve wrote: "We had a political stir during these days, nearly every soldier being hot for Lincoln. My own pen was prolific in articles for the home paper, one such article appearing as an editorial. The re-election of Lincoln had a great effect with both armies; it strengthened and solidified ours and correspondingly demoralized the enemy's, as an ever increasing desertion from their ranks testified."

Of a reception in the East Room of the White House he wrote: "Many attended including Maj. Meserve and wife; as I marched by Mr. Lincoln he seized my hand and so I received the presidential handshake of Abraham Lincoln, 'Ustatia's' greatest." And of a later date was this record: "April 14, towards midnight, I was aroused and commanded to man the intrenchments with my battalion. In a few minutes I was in saddle and but a short time after my breastworks were alive with men instructed to let no man pass unchallenged. With such orders came the news of President Lincoln's assassination."

William Neal Meserve went into the battle of Antietam a raw recruit and came out a veteran, his disabled left arm in a sling, only six men of his company answering roll call. "Company K went into this battle with about 60 men; 16 were killed and between 30 and 40 wounded, including three officers . . . thirteen of the sixteen dead wrapped in their blankets found a common grave." On November 19, with Burnside's army at Falmouth opposite Fredericksburg, having marched fifteen miles a day, his shoes had given out. "My bare feet would have touched the ground but for sundry handkerchiefs and rags. It was both inconvenient and painful." Through the thinning lines of the charge on Marye's Heights in the battle of Fredericksburg he lived to answer roll call, to sleep in mud that froze and changed back to mud during rainstorms. "Many a night my teeth chattered for hours. Days and nights together I did not get warm . . . wood was hard to get and green at that."

Later in 1863, after a short furlough home, he saw service in Kentucky and with Burnside at the siege of Knoxville, under Sherman's army at Vicksburg and in the march on Jackson, Mississippi. A captain now, it interested him that in action at Jackson he meets one of his men: "Stephenson, struck in the foot, who lest he should be shot in the back, as he said, hobbled off the field backward into safety." While in the field a box arrived for the captain by express. He opened it to find a sword with his name etched on the blade, a present from his Sunday-school class in Boston.

William Neal Meserve served nearly four years in Union armies, taking wounds and fighting often in the front lines of bloody actions at Antietam, Fredericksburg, Vicksburg, the siege of Knoxville, the Wilderness, Cold Harbor, Petersburg. Then in June, 1865, Major Meserve at twenty-five years of age took up his studies in the theological seminary of the Congregational Church at Hartford, Connecticut. His first son, Frederick Hill Meserve, was born in November of that year. When Major Meserve finished his studies and graduated from the seminary, the American Missionary Association appointed him a missionary for the Pacific coast. To Oakland, California, he took with him his wife and three sons, a fourth son being born in Oakland. Up and down the State of California the Reverend Mr. Meserve rode, preaching and founding churches. In 1876 the family moved East and the father was pastor of a church in Frankford, Pennsylvania.

The family next moved to a pastorate in Boston, when young Frederick for a time studied medicine. The family moved to Colorado Springs, Colorado, and Frederick at twenty years of age took courses at Colorado College. In 1887 Harvard College appointed him its observer on Pikes Peak to determine if the Peak was a suitable place for an astronomical observatory in high altitude, the Harvard authorities deciding there were too many fogs and clouds on the Peak and Arequipa, Peru, was the better location. Ten months young Meserve spent on this assignment, half the time on the summit of Pikes Peak and half the time below. One six-week stretch he spent alone at the farthest height of the Peak. Snow, ice, and fierce winter winds stopped his one companion and cook from making that climb up those six weeks when Meserve couldn't climb down. The record for climbing this mountain was for a time held by Meserve. He walked the twenty miles from Colorado Springs to the Peak and twenty miles back in eleven and a half hours, a rise in altitude of from five to fourteen thousand feet. The winter of 1887 and the summer of 1888 were thus spent in the cause of astronomy, meteorology, and more and better weather predictions.

Next, at twenty-five years of age Meserve had his eye on being an architect. He took three years at the Massachusetts Institute of Technology, partly earning his way by writing Institute news for the Boston papers the *Globe* and the *Herald*. Evenings he worked for an engineering company. When they offered him the position of Western manager at Denver, Salt Lake City, San Francisco, and Seattle, with eleven states for his territory, he saw chances. "I wanted to get ahead. I had an offer and couldn't turn it down." This is probably in the main the correct answer, though there is evidence to indicate that Meserve quit his classes and went into income-producing work partly because he wanted to help other people who needed him. He was president of the Class of '92 and left it without graduating and explains it away with saying he couldn't turn down a good offer made him. Possibly the work into which he was thrown counted for as much as he would have got at M.I.T. Colorado Springs had him as assistant city civil engineer. Pikes Peak Railroad and the Colorado Midland Railway had him as surveyor. A real-estate firm put him to making maps and laying out two new towns between Manitou and Colorado Springs, supplying the architectural designs and blueprints. It was a pleasant aside that in the course of social affairs in Colorado Springs he chanced to meet a likable woman known to her friends as "Winnie," a daughter of Jefferson Davis, President of the Confederate States of America. Also in this period Meserve had fun as a horse wrangler: "I used to rope cattle just as any other cowboy did— could throw a steer riding at full speed." Meserve's physical build is that of the wiry, well-knit cowboy at home on the upper deck of a cayuse or a roan mustang.

The East called, and in 1893 he took desk with Deering, Milliken & Company, a textile commission house. He has stayed fifty years and is still there, though he made a little detour of five years when he had a seat on the New York Stock Exchange and was a partner in the brokerage firm of Charles W. Turner & Company. Manuals of corporation directorates show Meserve listed as a director in woolen mill companies of Maine, in cotton mill corporations of the South, a bleachery in New York State, and other concerns, including a distributing chain known as The Mercantile Stores Company, of which he is vice-president and director. He is a member of the Cotton Exchange of New York, eats regularly at the Merchants Club, and attends sessions of the Loyal Legion, whose membership consists of Union Army officers and their sons.

His wife he found in a white wooden-frame house at the corner of Park Avenue and Eighty-third Street, and in 1899 she, Edith Turner, at nineteen, married him. Among their blessings they count two daughters and a son, five granddaughters, and four grandsons.

When Meserve looks back at his life and asks what got him first going in the collection of photographs, he recalls that his father had written in neat script a manuscript titled "A Personal Record," taken mostly from a diary the father kept during his service in the Civil War. "I thought it would be appropriate to illustrate this family keepsake with some Civil War photographs," says Meserve. "I was thirty-five years old when I went to a book auction in Bangs Auction Room in lower Fifth Avenue. A packet of fifty photographs was offered, with no examination of it permitted to bidders. My bid was so low that I don't like to mention it. The packet was knocked down to me at an absurd figure. Not long after I was bid for a single print in that packet a sum one hundred times what I had paid for the entire fifty in the packet. I got into the habit of going to auctions and of studying catalogues."

His interest in the Lincoln era and its camera record grew and deepened. One day he called at the New York office of E. & H. T. Anthony & Company. That firm had in storage a collection of original portrait negatives made by Mathew B. Brady in his New York and Washington galleries. That great camera worker had, with a corps of assistants, at his own expense made the first extended series of photographs of a modern war—the men, the weapons, the horses, the landscapes, private soldiers and generals, political leaders, women and children. From E. & H. T. Anthony & Company Brady bought most of his photographic chemicals and supplies, and had run deep into debt. His faith in the camera record of the war ran high. The debts piled up. He could hear the rats of bankruptcy gnawing in the still midnights. But he went on. He would serve history and his country. He would prove what photography could do by telling what neither the tongues nor the letters of soldiers could tell of troops in camp, on the march, or mute and bullet-riddled on the ground. He went on, possibly aware that his own name was standing high and deathless along with the testimony of his thousands of glass negatives. The Federal Government during the war refused appropriations for his work, yet later did go so far as to pay $25,000 for part of his prints and negatives. Also Brady had continued his portrait gallery. But the huge outlays he had made for his war photographs still kept him in debt. And Brady died forgotten and penniless in a New York hospital, the tributes to him as an artist and the true measure of his contribution to history and American culture to come from later generations.

"It is not too well known how E. & H. T. Anthony came to own these portrait negatives and publish them as the successors of Mathew B. Brady," says Meserve. "But these are the original negatives that I acquired from the successors of those who had them from Brady and once advertised them widely. The day of the family album had passed and the stored negatives were waiting for a new owner to bring them to life."

Meserve went to Hoboken, to the second story of an old warehouse, and found two-foot piles of negatives dusty and crisscrossed, scores of broken negatives, and a young representative of Anthony & Company saying: "I wish you'd buy these. They're in the way here." This is when Meserve picked off the floor and held to the light a negative of Abraham Lincoln. A few days later Meserve's young wife, in their house at Madison Avenue and Seventy-fifth Street, got a surprise. She knew her husband had some articles arriving from Hoboken. But she did not expect two big vans and a basement room nearly filled with big boxes of glass negatives. So Meserve came home that night and began unpacking his acquisition of from fifteen thousand to eighteen thousand negatives, in size mostly cartes de visite. Of this period his daughter Dorothy [1] recalls: "Father and Mother sat in this basement room evening after evening, Mother quietly knitting or sewing, Father digging through his finds, pausing to examine and learn, then digging in again, wondering, discovering what he had. I remember as a small child taking it for granted that after I went to bed I must be very quiet and not call, for it was a long climb upstairs."

Another time when the moving vans startled Mrs. Meserve with their cargo, purchased by her unpredictable husband, they left in the basement thirty thousand photographs of stage people. This lot with others now has run to a total above fifty thousand photographs, many of them "cabinet-style," presenting actors, actresses, singers, dancers, vaudevillians, from early

[1] Dorothy Meserve Kunhardt (Mrs. Philip B. Kunhardt of Morristown, New Jersey) gave valuable assistance and helpful suggestions in the preparation and editing of the manuscripts and texts of this book.

1840 through the late 1890's. Bit by bit and lot by lot Meserve's collection ran to upward of two hundred thousand photographs.

In 1917 Meserve completed four sets of privately printed books, twenty-eight volumes to the set, four photographs on each page. Looking at this row of books and handling them, for they are heavy, and taking note that the four pictures to each page are not engraver's half-tones but genuine photographic prints, you don't know whether it is supercolossal or just plain colossal. About eight thousand names and faces, forms now faded that shared in the making of American history and culture from the 1840's to the early 1900's. "Who do you want?" asks Meserve with a twinkling eye. "Name him. Or name her." Four of these twenty-eight volume sets he made. The purchasers were Samuel V. Hoffman, then president of the New York Historical Society, John Gribbel, a Philadelphia merchant and collector, the New York State Library in Albany, the Widener Library at Harvard University. In 1943 Meserve began work on a fifth twenty-eight volume set to be delivered to Indiana University, and a sixth which is to travel to the West coast and belong to Washington University, Pullman, Washington.

Of the early 1900's Meserve says: "After a year or two I had fifty Lincoln photographs. I was six or seven years getting one hundred put together. The next eight photographs of Lincoln took me seven years to gather. And the next eight required twenty-one years."

In 1911 Meserve published privately the first book titled *The Photographs of Abraham Lincoln*, on heavy rag paper, with durable boards, cased, the type large bold-face, the pages wide-margined, $35 a copy, and the edition limited to one hundred copies. Both the eagerness and the humility of Meserve are suggested in a prefatory paragraph in this volume: "No serious attempt has heretofore been made to collect and publish in chronological order the life photographs of Abraham Lincoln. It has been difficult to trace their history, and in some cases no accurate data exist of their time and place. It is not claimed that the portraits herein described are all located with absolute correctness, nor that all that exist are here listed; but it is not likely that there are many unpublished photographs. The attempt has been to make the work as correct and complete as may be at this time, and credit is freely given to those who have supplemented the very limited sources of information."

Subscribers to this book included collectors of Lincolniana keen and incessant in their hunt for new items. They saw Meserve and his work as highly useful, even momentous. They threw in with him. When they got a Lincoln photograph they compared it with those in the Meserve book, gave it the Meserve serial number. And if they couldn't find it in Meserve, they sent him the original or a copy, saying, "This looks like a new one," and awaited the reply sure to come from Meserve. He became the man best known for unquenchable interest in Lincoln photographs, from year to year unfailing in his researches and cumulative findings. During some forty years he has been a one-man bureau of information, a central office of inquiry and discovery, an important unofficial recorder and transmitter of Lincoln photographs and verified data thereto related. Quiet, modest, and unassuming, openly free-handed with friends and ungrudgingly generous with strangers, Meserve might be termed "a born natural" in his particular field.

Meserve refers to himself as a businessman. He is a scholar, of course, but makes no claims to scholarship. He was pleased at receiving the degree of Doctor of Letters from Lincoln Memorial University at Harrogate, Tennessee, though he would probably have been ready to trade the degree for just one more hitherto unknown Lincoln photograph. In politics he is a lifelong Republican-party man with partisan hates and loyalties. His hates are tempered, however, and his face shines with goodwill and humor. Children come to him to hear about the iron dog on the lawn of his grandfather's house in Dover, New Hampshire. "He barked whenever he heard the doorbell ring. You may not believe it, but that iron dog did bark whenever he heard the doorbell ring." But you should also know that because he never heard the doorbell ring he never barked.

From his long-time friend Charles W. McLellan, whose collection of Lincolniana was bought by John D. Rockefeller, Jr., for permanent location at Brown University, Meserve heard this anecdote of a visit McLellan made to the Lincoln home before the Civil War. "McLellan told me he called at the Lincoln house. And while he was there he saw Mrs. Lincoln come downstairs holding her apron full of photographs and saying to Mr. Lincoln, 'Father, I'm sick and tired of these. I'm going to throw them away.' And Mr. Lincoln said, 'Oh, no, Mother, I wouldn't do that. Someone may want them some day.'"

THE PHOTOGRAPHS OF
ABRAHAM LINCOLN

by FREDERICK HILL MESERVE

The form and features of Abraham Lincoln are well known. He was perhaps the most-photographed American of his time. As many as one hundred and twenty different photographic portraits of Lincoln are known to us, all but three made during the last eight years of his life, when he was of national importance. Few of the original daguerreotypes and negatives are extant. These are priceless items.

How some of these valuable life documents of Lincoln have disappeared is known. Two negatives made by Alexander Hesler after the nomination in 1860 were destroyed in the Chicago fire of 1871, but fortunately prints had been made and circulated.

Leonard W. Volk at the time he made casts of Mr. Lincoln's hands in Springfield, on the Sunday after his nomination to the Presidency, is said to have made three negatives, but so far as is known no prints were made from them, and they were lost in the Boston fire of 1872. One of the ambrotypes made at Macomb, Illinois, in 1858 came into the possession of Mr. Richard Watson Gilder, the editor of the *Century Magazine*, but Mr. Gilder told the present writer it was lost in a fire in the office of the Century Company in New York. The last negative made of the President, in the week of his death, one of a series taken by Alexander Gardner, was cracked. After only one print was made from this broken negative the glass plate was shattered by its owner as defective and of no value. This single, priceless photographic print was bought from Gardner in 1874 by Mr. Truman H. Bartlett, the sculptor and author. Later it came into the collection of the present writer.

A life mask of Mr. Lincoln was made by Leonard W. Volk in Chicago in 1860. Copies of this mask in plaster and bronze, supplemented by the photographs, have formed the basis of many statues of Lincoln that have been erected. Clark Mills made a life mask of Mr. Lincoln in Washington in February, 1865, but it was a poor representation, and has been incorrectly called a death mask.

Of the countless engravings and paintings of Lincoln many are mere caricatures. The photographs show him as he was. The camera supplies exact portraiture. The daguerreotype, ambrotype, and ferrotype or "tintype" permitted only one portrait for each exposure, this being known as "positive" photography. Such early portraits are heirlooms. Collectors have eagerly sought them. Then the single-plate "positive" camera portrait gave way to glass negatives from which any number of prints could be made whenever wanted. At once photography became universal.

Sitting for a picture in the early days was an event. Itinerant daguerreotypists visited the small towns. Lincoln is recorded as having more than once entered a traveling studio to "have his picture taken" for an admiring friend.

The earliest portrait of Lincoln is a daguerreotype said to have been made in Springfield in 1846 when he was thirty-seven years old. Mr. Robert Todd Lincoln, who owned it, stated to the present writer that he believed it was made in Washington in 1848, when his father was a Representative in Congress. This portrait shows the rising lawyer of Springfield, Illinois, in the later 1840's. About ten years passed before Alexander Hesler made the second portraits of Lincoln in Chicago.

Before his election Mr. Lincoln's face was unbearded. After he began to grow a beard late in 1860 he never let the barber's razor travel over his cheeks and chin. His face was thin, and showed great kindliness of expression. The nose was prominent, cheeks somewhat sunken, eyes deep-set, the eyebrows well marked, the lips full. In some portraits the lid of one eye is noticeably lower than the other. In no photograph of Lincoln is the mouth open, even slightly. A mole on the right side of his face near the mouth is seen in all his full-face photographs. The marked lines about the mouth, even in his early portraits, deepened when the cares of state and the burdens of war came upon him. All his pictures show a full head of hair, and never closely cut as was the fashion of the time; it was parted generally upon the left side, but occasionally upon the right, and was brushed with little care. Once, it is said, he ran his fingers through his hair before the photographic plate was exposed.

Lincoln gave his own height as six feet three and one-half inches in his stocking feet. He carried his shoulders slightly bent, as is usual with very tall men. His attitudes in the photographs are those of repose. If his movements were awkward, there is no hint of it in the photographs, which speak of dignity. Some of his early portraits do not show great care in dress, as though he went to the camera sitting without special preparation. At one time after a speech in his shirt sleeves on a hot day, he visited a photograph gallery at the request of friends and borrowed the artist's coat for the picture. His early pictures show his neck in the high stock. In all the later ones he is shown with the turnover collar and black bow tie. The only personal ornament he permitted himself, as shown by the photographs, was a watch chain. This was presented to him by a California delegation which came to the White House to promote the building of the transcontinental railroad. It is now owned by Mr. Oliver R. Barrett of Chicago, who says: "It appears to be composed of hair, but in reality it is of solid gold of the finest workmanship in the form of a woven or braided hair chain."

Three portraits of the Lincoln Springfield home, taken at two different times with the camera placed on the opposite side of the street, show the figure of Lincoln. Two photographs of the group on the platform at Independence Hall in Philadelphia were made during a brief speech at a flag-raising at dawn on February 22, 1861. Seven photographs by Mathew B. Brady were made at the time of his visit in October, 1862, to General George B. McClellan at Antietam, Maryland, after the battle. One of these in a group of generals shows his height, his tall hat adding to the effect. A photograph of the general inauguration scene fronting the Capitol was made in 1861, but the figure of Lincoln is not distinguishable. Two photographs were made by Alexander Gardner at the time of his second inauguration in 1865, one showing him seated beside Vice-President Johnson, and the other as he delivered his inaugural speech. These are two of the few photographs of Mr. Lincoln in the open air. There was no posing. His attitude was invariably natural. The real Lincoln seems to be shown in these outdoor photographs.

Twelve photographs, not counting those where his figure is small, show him standing. These have helped many sculptors.

No portraits or group pictures made of Mr. Lincoln and Senator Douglas show these orators in their seven political debates in 1858. It is believed that the first photographs of any President or President-elect speaking to the people are those showing Mr. Lincoln at Philadelphia on the journey to Washington in 1861. At the National Cemetery at Gettysburg on November 19, 1863, when the President read the few words of his address, a photographer set up his camera and was preparing to photograph the celebrities on the platform. Lincoln's short speech was over, however, before the man was ready, and the only pictures obtained showed the backs of people in the dispersing crowd.

Mr. Lincoln's first visit to the studios of Mathew B. Brady, who was later to make so many photographs of him as President, was on February 27, 1860, the day of his Cooper Institute speech in New York. The portraits then made at the request of the Young Men's Central Republican Union are the best known of all likenesses made before he became President. It has been said, perhaps with exaggeration, that over one hundred thousand copies were distributed in the campaign later in the year. Mr. Lincoln himself said that this speech and these photographs helped him to the White House. Originals of these portraits, however, are scarce items in Lincoln collections.

Mr. Lincoln arrived in Washington for the inauguration on February 23, 1861, and on the same day, in Brady's other studio, six sitting photographs were made showing the whole figure facing to the right. The studio properties, especially one chair, used in these pictures will be seen in many later portraits and identify Brady's work.

In 1863 a series of photographs of the President was made at Mr. Lincoln's own request. Alexander Gardner and his son James, formerly employed by Brady, were about to open a gallery of their own. They had previously worked in a small building on the White House grounds, where President Lincoln had visited and made friends with them, saying he would be their first sitter. The day before the gallery opened to the public, on a Sunday morning, at least nine different negatives were made.

No known photographs show President Lincoln with his Cabinet or any member of it, although it has been said that he was photographed by Brady with Secretary of State William H. Seward. The figures in the celebrated painting by Francis B. Carpenter of Lincoln and his Cabinet at the signing of the Emancipation Proclamation were made from separate photographs, for the most part by Brady. Brady also made, at Mr. Carpenter's request, two photographs of Lincoln, one sitting and one standing, at the table upon which the Proclamation was signed. In one of these Mr. Nicolay, a private secretary to the President, and the painter himself sit in the chairs to be occupied in the painting by Mr. Seward and Mr. Stanton.

The profile photographs of Mr. Lincoln made by Brady early in 1864, showing the right side of his face, are perhaps the best known of the few profile portraits. Of the nine different negatives made at this time, six of the glass plates which were in the camera are now part of the ten original Brady negatives in the Meserve Collection.

Both Brady and Gardner made photographs of President Lincoln with Thomas (Tad), the son who was his father's fondest companion. There seem to be no photographs of family groups, and Mr. Robert Todd Lincoln told the present writer that his father and mother were never photographed together. A contemporary engraving showed Mr. and Mrs. Lincoln standing together, but the figures had been copied from two separate photographs. Mrs. Lincoln, very much shorter than the President, was made to appear perhaps six to eight inches taller than she really was. The well-known group of the Lincoln family painted by Carpenter in the third year of the Administration shows Tad standing by his father, who has an open book on his knees. This pose of the two appears to have been copied by the artist from a photograph by Brady. This original glass negative is also in the present writer's collection. The book on Mr. Lincoln's knees is a photograph album which was in Brady's studio, and not the Bible, as some have asserted. In one of these photographs of the President and Tad Mrs. Lincoln's figure appears, but it is clearly a mechanical addition.

On Monday, April 10, 1865, in the week of his assassination, the last photographs of Mr. Lincoln were made by Alexander Gardner, including one of the President with Tad. The President had been visiting General Grant at City Point, Virginia, and on Sunday, April 9, while the articles of surrender of General Robert E. Lee's army were being signed at Appomattox, Mr. Lincoln aboard a steamboat was making his way to Washington. He arrived late in the afternoon and immediately went to the bedside of Secretary of State William H. Seward, who had leaped from a carriage when his horses ran away a few days before.

Two photographs were made in New York of the body of Lincoln by Gurney, a well-known photographer, as it lay in state in the City Hall on the journey to Springfield. War Department documents indicate that the negatives were destroyed on the orders of Mr. Edwin M. Stanton, Secretary of War, at the insistence of Mrs. Lincoln.

Although the camera did not record Lincoln in animated and spectacular moments, it has left a series of portraits of the grave and reflective Lincoln, which students of history and admirers of Lincoln will cherish.

In 1911 the writer published privately, in an edition of one hundred copies, a volume containing one hundred photographic portraits of Lincoln, and later two supplements of eight portraits each. An attempt was made with the records then available to arrange the first hundred portraits in chronological order. Later research by the writer, with much valuable aid from students and collectors, has materially changed this first order; but although the portraits in this book are given the chronological order as last determined, the original numbering has been retained, as the portraits have become more or less identified with the numbers first used.

During the more than forty years of his search for the photographs of Lincoln the writer has become indebted to many collectors and students for invaluable aid. These offered photographs to be copied and gave the names and dates from their own studies. Few of them are living today, but the mention of their names would be a list of all the great Lincoln students whose collections have been broken up or have become additions to university and other libraries. Mr. Oliver R. Barrett of Chicago is one whose researches today are indispensable to all students. Miss Ida M. Tarbell, who gave her manuscripts to Allegheny College, never failed to contribute her intimate knowledge in the search for facts. Mr. R. Gerald McMurtry of Lincoln Memorial University has in a brief time gathered a wealth of information for the student, Dr. Harry E. Pratt, formerly the secretary of the Abraham Lincoln Association of Springfield, himself an author, is a friend of all collectors. Dr. F. Lauriston Bullard, formerly chief editorial writer of the *Boston Herald*, president of the Lincoln Group of Boston, has a vast and exact knowledge, and offers it gladly. Mr. Paul Angle, the Librarian of the Illinois State Historical Library at Springfield, a prolific writer of history, has been a helper of many besides the present writer. And Dr. Louis A. Warren, editor and lecturer, director of the Lincoln National Life Foundation of Fort Wayne, Indiana, who has built up an enormous collection of Lincolniana, has over many years given his historical resources to aid in the study and revision of the writer's work. These are some only of those who are carrying on the historical study of Lincoln and his times. They are the living successors of Judge Daniel Fish of Minneapolis, Major William H. Lambert of Philadelphia, Mr. Judd Stewart of New York, and Mr. Charles W. McLellan of Champlain, New York. Of this group the writer was a younger associate, now with grateful memory of fellowship with them.

Lastly, great credit is due to Mr. J. A. Walton, a New York photographer, who during forty years has made more than a quarter-million prints from the Meserve historical negatives. In all this time only one important glass negative was broken, one of Mrs. Lincoln; this was put together and used, although the crack is visible.

In connection with the reproduction of the photographs in this book, it should be stated that there has been no touching-up or removing of blemishes in order to make more perfect pictures. Some of the rarest portraits appear to be the poorest, but the original photographs in the Meserve Collection in all cases have been copied with absolute fidelity.

I

The earliest known portrait of Abraham Lincoln. A photograph of
the daguerreotype believed to have been made by N. H. Shepherd in
Springfield, Illinois, in 1846. Mr. Robert Todd Lincoln, who owned the
original, stated to the author that he believed it was made in Washington about 1848, when his father was a Representative in Congress.

6

101

A photograph made by Alexander Hesler in Chicago, February, 1857. Known as the first Hesler photograph. It was used in the Lincoln-Douglas senatorial campaign. The negative is said to have been lost in the Chicago fire of 1871.

A photograph made by Alexander Hesler in Chicago, February, 1857. This and Number 6 were evidently made at the same time. The history of the negative is not known. There is a legend that Lincoln deliberately mussed up his hair before these portraits were made.

5

A photograph of the ambrotype made by Samuel G. Alschuler in Urbana, Illinois, in April, 1858. Miss Ida M. Tarbell in *The Early Life of Abraham Lincoln* stated that his linen duster was exchanged for the smaller dark coat of the photographer.

17

A photograph of the ambrotype believed to have been made by Preston Butler in Springfield in 1858. *McClure's Magazine* of March, 1896, stated it was copied from a carbon enlargement of the ambrotype of June, 1860, but the style of collar worn by Mr. Lincoln seems to place it in the earlier year.

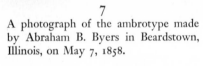

7

A photograph of the ambrotype made by Abraham B. Byers in Beardstown, Illinois, on May 7, 1858.

3

A photograph of the daguerreotype made by P. Von Schneider in Chicago in July, 1858. Mr. Lincoln spoke in Chicago on July 10, 1858, to answer Senator Stephen A. Douglas, who had spoken there the day before.

IO

A photograph of the ambrotype made by W. P. Pearson in Macomb, Illinois, August 26, 1858, five days after the first debate with Senator Stephen A. Douglas at Ottawa, Illinois. The ambrotype was last owned in 1888 by Mr. Richard Watson Gilder, editor of the *Century Magazine*, when it was lost in the fire of the Century Building in New York.

II

A photograph of the ambrotype made by W. P. Pearson in Macomb, Illinois, August 28, 1858. Slightly different from Number 10. There is a similar photograph with the imprint of S. P. Tresize, a photographer of Springfield, but probably a copy of the ambrotype.

12

A photograph of the ambrotype made by Calvin Jackson, an itinerant ambrotypist in Pittsfield, Illinois, on October 1, 1858, six days before the fifth debate with Senator Stephen A. Douglas at Galesburg, Illinois.

13

A photograph of the ambrotype made by William Judkins Thompson at Monmouth, Illinois, on October 11, 1858, two days before the sixth debate with Senator Stephen A. Douglas at Quincy, Illinois. Mr. Lincoln spoke for three hours at Monmouth.

14

A photograph of the ambrotype made by H. H. Cole, probably in 1859 in Peoria, Illinois. Major William H. Lambert of Philadelphia in 1902 bought the ambrotype from Mr. Guy W. Hubbard of Springfield, who stated that in 1862 it had been given to his father, Captain William A. Hubbard of the 17th Illinois Infantry, for an act of bravery.

15

A photograph of the ambrotype made by H. H. Cole, probably in 1859, in Peoria, Illinois. Slightly different from Number 14. Copied from a small tintype on a contemporary campaign badge.

8

A photograph probably made by S. M. Fassett in Chicago in October, 1859. Mr. Truman H. Bartlett of Boston stated in 1910 in connection with his copy, "Alexander Hesler of Chicago says he took this photograph in 1858." It is considered one of the best of the beardless photographs.

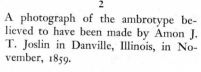

A photograph of the ambrotype believed to have been made by Amon J.
T. Joslin in Danville, Illinois, in November, 1859.

A photograph of an ambrotype, probably made before 1860, about which
there is no information.

18

19

A photograph believed to have been made in New York on February 27, 1860, by Mathew B. Brady, photographer following the Union armies during the war years.

A photograph made in the New York studio of Mathew B. Brady on February 27, 1860. It is very slightly different from Number 20.

20

A photograph by Mathew B. Brady made in New York on February 27, 1860. It is known as the Cooper Institute portrait, having been made on the day Lincoln delivered his speech under the auspices of the Young Men's Central Republican Union. This and the two preceding portraits are the first made by Brady.

21

22

A photograph of the ambrotype made by William Church in Springfield on May 20, 1860, two days after Lincoln's nomination for President. This and Numbers 22 and 109 are believed to be the first portraits made of Lincoln after his nomination.

A photograph of the ambrotype made by William Church in Springfield on May 20, 1860. This portrait, with Numbers 21 and 109, had no wide circulation, as they were made for Mr. J. Henry Brown of Philadelphia, who used them in painting a portrait of the nominee.

109

A photograph of the ambrotype made by William Church in Springfield on May 20, 1860, at the same time as Numbers 21 and 22.

4

A photograph of a ferrotype believed to have been made in 1860. Miss Ida M. Tarbell published this portrait in *The Early Life of Abraham Lincoln* in 1896, believing it was made about 1856. The photographer is not known.

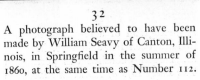

32

A photograph believed to have been made by William Seavy of Canton, Illinois, in Springfield in the summer of 1860, at the same time as Number 112.

112

A photograph made by William Seavy of Canton, Illinois, in Springfield in the summer of 1860. The negative was lost when the Seavy Gallery burned.

III

A photograph by an unknown photographer, probably made in the
summer of 1860. It may be the portrait known to have been made for
Leonard W. Volk, the sculptor, who visited Mr. Lincoln the day
after his nomination and made casts of his hands.

102

A photograph by Joseph Hill made in Springfield in June, 1860. Mr. Hill stated that this print is from one of four negatives, all of which were destroyed by fire.

31

A photograph by an unknown photographer, probably made in Springfield in the summer of 1860.

25

A photograph by Alexander Hesler
made in Springfield on June 3, 1860.
Mr. George B. Ayres after Hesler's
death in 1865 obtained this negative
and Number 26, which were of cabinet size, and touched up 8″ x 10″ negatives made from the originals. They
had a very wide distribution. In recent
years these negatives were damaged in
the mails; they are now in the Smith-
sonian Institution.

26

A photograph by Alexander Hesler
made in Springfield on June 3, 1860.
The purchase of this negative and
Number 25 by Mr. George B. Ayres
doubtless saved them from loss in the
Hesler Gallery, which was burned in
the Chicago fire of 1871.

27

28

A photograph by Alexander Hesler made in Springfield on June 3, 1860. Mr. Robert Todd Lincoln gave to the compiler small copies of this portrait and Number 28 which had not been enlarged and touched up, as were Numbers 25 and 26 of this series. The negative was said to have been lost in the Chicago fire of 1871.

A photograph by Alexander Hesler made in Springfield on June 3, 1860. This and Number 27 did not have the wide distribution of Numbers 25 and 26, and are little known except to collectors. The negative is said to have been lost in the Chicago fire of 1871.

110

A photograph by an unknown photographer, probably made in Springfield in the summer of 1860.

113

A photograph by an unknown photographer, probably made in Springfield in the summer of 1860. A nearly
similar portrait was made by Tresize's
Enterprise Gallery in Springfield.

29

A photograph of the 4″ x 5″ ambrotype
made by Preston Butler in Springfield
on August 13, 1860, for Mr. J. Henry
Brown, who used it to make a minia-
ture on ivory which later was owned
by Mr. Robert Todd Lincoln.

30

A photograph of the 4″ x 5″ ambrotype
made by Preston Butler in Springfield
on August 13, 1860. It is likely that this
portrait was made for the same purpose
as was Number 29. Both are scarce
items of Lincolniana.

23

Enlarged detail of a large photograph made in Springfield by A. J. Whipple of Boston, probably during the 1860 campaign. With Mr. Lincoln is one of the younger sons inside the fence at the corner of his home. The picture was taken from across the street and took in the whole house.

24

Enlarged detail of a large photograph made by A. J. Whipple of Boston in Springfield at the same time as Number 23. Both of the younger sons are seen. The boy indistinctly seen on the sidewalk is Isaac R. Diller, a playmate of the Lincoln boys, who died in Springfield on September 28, 1943, in his eighty-ninth year.

16

Detail of an 8″ x 10″ photograph of the Lincoln home in Springfield by an unknown photographer, showing Lincoln standing in the door with a crowd of neighbors, watching a procession, probably in the summer of 1860. A procession is known to have passed his house on August 8, 1860. It appears to be a demonstration favoring the admission of Kansas to the Union, as a banner states, "Won't you let me in? (Kansas)"

120

A photograph in the Ida M. Tarbell Collection at Allegheny College, Meadville, Pennsylvania. On the back of the cabinet-size photograph Major William H. Lambert, the eminent collector of Lincolniana, wrote: "Lincoln in 1860. Copy of an old print in possession of J. Howard Brown, Philadelphia. Found among the effects of the late J. Henry Brown, artist, who painted a likeness of the President in 1860."

9

A photograph of the daguerreotype believed to have been made by C. S. German in Springfield in 1860. Major William H. Lambert of Philadelphia, who owned the original, was unable to give the compiler its history, but he believed it was made in 1858.

33

A photograph made by Samuel G. Al-schuler in Springfield in November, in 1860. This is believed to be the first photograph showing the beard, which is seen in all later photographs.

34

A photograph made by C. S. German in Springfield, January 26, 1861. The original negative of cabinet size is in the Lincoln Collection of Dr. Herbert Wells Fay of Springfield. The portrait for the original ten-dollar greenback was engraved from this photograph.

35

Enlarged directly from a negative believed to be the original by C. S. German made in Springfield in February, 1861, now in the Meserve Collection. This and the next portrait are believed to be the last portraits of Lincoln before he left for Washington to be inaugurated President of the United States.

36

A photograph made by C. S. German in Springfield in February, 1861, at the same time as Number 35.

103

A detail from a large photograph made by F. D. Richards in Philadelphia on February 22, 1861, at a flag-raising at Independence Hall at sunrise at which the President-elect spoke briefly, leaving before the exercises were over. Mr. Lincoln may be seen directly above the single star to the left in the flag draped over the railing of the platform. Another photograph was made of the group after Mr. Lincoln left.

37

A detail from a large photograph made by F. D. Richards in Philadelphia on February 22, 1861, at a flag-raising at Independence Hall at sunrise. In this picture Mr. Lincoln is standing directly over the third star from the left in the flag draped over the railing of the platform. This and Number 103 are believed to be the first photographs of a President-elect or a President speaking.

68

A photograph by Mathew B. Brady made in Washington on February 23, 1861, the day the President-elect arrived for the inauguration. The original glass negative, different from Number 118, is in the Meserve Collection.

118

A photograph by Mathew B. Brady made in Washington on February 23, 1861, the day the President-elect arrived for the inauguration. The original glass negative, different from Number 68, is in the Meserve Collection.

69

A photograph by Mathew B. Brady made in Washington on February 23, 1861.

70

A photograph by Mathew B. Brady
made in Washington February 23, 1861.

71

A photograph by Mathew B. Brady
made in Washington February 23, 1861.

72

A photograph by Mathew B. Brady made in Washington February 23, 1861.

42

A photograph by Mathew B. Brady made in Washington before October 1, 1861. On that date the President gave it to Mrs. Lucy G. Speed, the mother of James Speed and Joshua F. Speed, all his early friends.

38

A photograph by Mathew B. Brady, believed to have been made in
1862. The original glass negative is in the Meserve Collection.

62

A photograph by Mathew B. Brady
believed to have been made in 1862.
Slightly different from Number 63.

63

A photograph by Mathew B. Brady
believed to have been made in 1862.

64
A photograph by Mathew B. Brady
believed to have been made in 1862.

65
A photograph by Mathew B. Brady
believed to have been made in 1862.

66

A photograph by Mathew B. Brady
believed to have been made in 1862.

67

A photograph by Mathew B. Brady
believed to have been made in 1862.

43

Detail from an 8″ x 10″ photograph made by Mathew B. Brady about October 2, 1862, as the President sat in General George B. McClellan's tent at Antietam, Maryland, after the battle.

44

Detail from an 8″ x 10″ photograph made by Mathew B. Brady about October 2, 1862, when the President visited General George B. Mc-Clellan at his headquarters, Antietam, Maryland.

104

Detail from an 8″ x 10″ photograph made by Mathew B. Brady about October 2, 1862, as the President sat in General George B. McClellan's tent at Antietam, Maryland. Different from Number 43.

47

Detail from an 8″ x 10″ photograph made by Mathew B. Brady about October 2, 1862, when the President visited General George B. McClellan at his headquarters at Antietam, Maryland.

45

Detail from an 8″ x 10″ photograph made by Mathew B. Brady about October 2, 1862, at Antietam, Maryland. Major General John A. McClernand and Major Allan Pinkerton of the Secret Service are with the President.

46

Detail from an 8″ x 10″ photograph made by Mathew B. Brady about October 2, 1862, at Antietam, Maryland. Major General John A. McClernand and Major Allan Pinkerton are with the President.

48

Detail from an 8″ x 10″ photograph made by Mathew B. Brady about October 2, 1862, at Antietam, Maryland. In this and Number 47 Mr. John W. Garrett, president of the Baltimore & Ohio Railroad, is shown. Copied from a photograph which had been touched up.

55

A photograph made by Alexander Gardner on August 9, 1863, the day before the new gallery of the Gardner Brothers was opened to the public.

49
A photograph made by Alexander
Gardner on August 9, 1863.

50
A photograph made by Alexander
Gardner on August 9, 1863.

51
A photograph made by Alexander
Gardner on August 9, 1863.

52
A photograph made by Alexander
Gardner on August 9, 1863.

53

A photograph made by Alexander Gardner on August 9, 1863. Nine different photographs are known to have been made at this time, the first made by Alexander and James Gardner, who had formerly been employed by Mathew B. Brady.

54
A photograph made by Alexander
Gardner on August 9, 1863.

114
A photograph made by Alexander
Gardner on August 9, 1863.

105
A photograph made by Alexander
Gardner on August 9, 1863.

61
A photograph made by Alexander
Gardner on November 8, 1863.

56

A photograph made by Alexander Gardner on November 8, 1863. The President is shown with his secretaries, John G. Nicolay and John Hay, who is standing.

58

A photograph made by Alexander Gardner on November 15, 1863, four days before the speech at Gettysburg. Mr. Noah Brooks in *Washington in Lincoln's Time* stated that Senator Edward Everett's oration to be delivered at Gettysburg was in an envelope, which may be seen on the table.

57

A photograph made by Alexander Gardner on November 15, 1863, four days before the speech at Gettysburg. Here, as in Number 58, the envelope containing Senator Everett's speech may be seen on the table.

59

A photograph made by Alexander Gardner on November 15, 1863. This portrait has been widely published and is perhaps the best-known full-face portrait of the President.

60

A photograph made by Alexander Gardner on November 15, 1863. This portrait, differing slightly from Number 59, is little known.

107

A photograph made by Mathew B. Brady in 1863, different from Number 75. An enlarged copy by Gurney & Son of New York was widely circulated.

73
A photograph by Mathew B. Brady,
believed to have been made in 1863.

74
A photograph by Mathew B. Brady
believed to have been made in 1863.

75
A photograph by Mathew B. Brady
believed to have been made in 1863.

115
A photograph by Mathew B. Brady
believed to have been made in 1863.

76
A photograph by Mathew B. Brady
believed to have been made in 1863.

77
A photograph by Mathew B. Brady
believed to have been made in 1863.

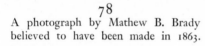

78

A photograph by Mathew B. Brady believed to have been made in 1863.

88

A photograph made by Thomas Walker, probably in 1863. Captain O. H. Oldroyd, the proprietor of the Lincoln Museum in the house on Tenth Street in Washington where Lincoln died, stated that Mr. Walker was an amateur photographer, an employee of the Treasury Department.

39

40

A photograph of the President and Thomas (Tad) made by Mathew B. Brady on February 9, 1864, as Mr. Lincoln looked at an album of photographs in Brady's studio. It was used by Mr. Francis B. Carpenter in the painting of the Lincoln family. The original glass negative is in the Meserve Collection.

A photograph by Mathew B. Brady similar to Number 39 that has been touched up and had a background added.

41

A photograph by Mathew B. Brady similar to Number 39, with Mrs. Lincoln mechanically added. Mr. Robert Todd Lincoln stated to the compiler that his father and mother were never photographed together.

86

A photograph made by Mathew B. Brady on February 9, 1864. The original glass negative is in the Meserve Collection.

81

A photograph made by Mathew B. Brady on February 9, 1864. This is one of the celebrated portraits known as the Brady profiles. The original glass negative is in the Meserve Collection.

83

A photograph made by Mathew B. Brady on February 9, 1864. This is copied from a photograph, and is slightly different from the others in this series.

82

A photograph made by Mathew B. Brady on February 9, 1864. This is one of the celebrated portraits known as the Brady profiles. The original glass negative is in the Meserve Collection.

84

A photograph made by Mathew B. Brady on February 9, 1864. This is one of the celebrated portraits known as the Brady profiles. The original glass negative is in the Meserve Collection.

119

A photograph made by Mathew B. Brady on February 9, 1864.

85

A photograph made by Mathew B. Brady on February 9, 1864. Mr. Robert Todd Lincoln stated to the compiler that he considered this to be the best photograph of his father. It is the most widely known of all the portraits of Lincoln, as it appears on the five-dollar bill.

87

A photograph made by Mathew B. Brady on February 9, 1864. The original glass negative is in the Meserve Collection.

108

A photograph made by Mathew B. Brady on February 9, 1864. The original glass negative is in the Meserve Collection.

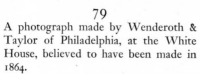

79

A photograph made by Wenderoth & Taylor of Philadelphia, at the White House, believed to have been made in 1864.

80

A photograph made by Wenderoth & Taylor of Philadelphia, at the White House, believed to have been made in 1864.

106

116

Detail from a photograph made by Mathew B. Brady on April 20, 1864. Mr. Henry Wolf, the engraver, who owned the original, stated that Mr. Francis B. Carpenter, the artist, said of it: "This photograph was made in the White House in 1864. The legs in the white trousers are those of Mr. Nicolay; the legs at Mr. Lincoln's right are my own."

Detail from a photograph made by Mathew B. Brady on April 20, 1864. Mr. Francis B. Carpenter, the artist, wrote on the back of the photograph that it was taken under his direction and that upon this table the Emancipation Proclamation was signed.

91

A photograph believed to have been made by Mathew B. Brady early in 1865.

92

A photograph believed to have been made by Mathew B. Brady early in 1865.

93

A photograph made by H. F. Warren of Waltham, Massachusetts, at the
White House on March 6, 1865.

89

Detail from an 8″ x 10″ photograph
made by Alexander Gardner of the
second inauguration of President Lincoln on March 4, 1865. The President
is sitting without a hat at the left of
the reading desk. On his right is Andrew Johnson, the Vice-President. The
Justices of the Supreme Court are at
the right of the reading desk.

90

Detail of an 8″ x 10″ photograph made by Alexander Gardner of the second inauguration of President Lincoln on March 4, 1865. The President is reading from his manuscript. Mr. Nicolay, one of his secretaries, is standing behind the empty chair. Vice-President Johnson's face is hidden by the hat held in his left hand.

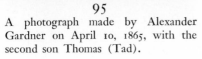

95

A photograph made by Alexander Gardner on April 10, 1865, with the second son Thomas (Tad).

96

A photograph made by Alexander Gardner on April 10, 1865, similar to Number 95, with a screen, showing the unfinished Washington Monument and the Potomac River, used as a background.

94

A photograph made by Alexander Gardner on April 10, 1865.

97

A photograph made by Alexander Gardner on April 10, 1865. The President is holding his glasses in his right hand.

98

A photograph made by Alexander Gardner on April 10, 1865.

99

A photograph made by Alexander Gardner on April 10, 1865.

100

A photograph made by Alexander Gardner on Monday, April 10, 1865. Mr. Truman H. Bartlett, the author and sculptor, acquired it from Mr. Gardner in 1874, who then stated that only one print was made from the large broken negative before it was considered value-less and destroyed, and that it was the last photograph made on that day. No later photographs were made of the President in life. This single print is in the Meserve Collection.

MRS. ABRAHAM LINCOLN
(Mary Todd)

ROBERT TODD LINCOLN   ROBERT TODD LINCOLN

WILLIAM WALLACE LINCOLN   WILLIAM WALLACE LINCOLN

THOMAS LINCOLN

THOMAS LINCOLN

MRS. LINCOLN WITH WILLIE
AND TAD

LOCKWOOD TODD WITH WILLIE
AND TAD

LIFE MASK OF ABRAHAM LINCOLN

MADE BY LEONARD W. VOLK, MARCH, 1860, CHICAGO

One of the earliest castings, in bronze. Purchased from the sculptor Truman H. Bartlett by Meserve. Loaned by Meserve for several months in 1925 for a photograph by Edward Steichen, who sought to bring full meaning to this bronze documentation of the flesh-and-bone structure of a face. "The photograph brings out more than the physical mask," said Oliver R. Barrett of Chicago in 1935. "The beholder may return to it many times across years and find its silence sacred and moving. It is a masterpiece of Lincoln portraiture, a supreme interpretation."   C. S.

PEOPLE WHO TOUCHED LINCOLN

Some touched him to bother him, others to bring him good news, bad news, messages wanting answers. Some touched him to hand him reports, announcements, warnings, data, memoranda, pens to write with, paper to write on, advice, threats. Some touched him to speak blessings and wish him peace and well-being, others to bear down on him with scorn and wrath, belittlement and backbiting. All have been witnesses for him, against him, or neither for nor against. Meserve has known some of them for years, talked long with them or had many letters from them, as with Robert Todd Lincoln, Horace Porter, Thomas T. Eckert, David Homer Bates. "They were the people who touched Lincoln," says Meserve. "We can't put them all in. The ninety faces here are nearly a crowd. Thirty or forty of them are permanently associated with Lincoln." A few saw him often, across years, like Herndon, Lamon, Nicolay, Hay, Brooks, Browning, in dress and undress, bowed with burdens or shaken with mirth. Others saw him briefly but saw much in those moments and wrote it vividly. Still others crossed his path definitely, to help or to hinder, and Lincoln read their faces and they were in his album of memory.

C. S.

SARAH BUSH LINCOLN
Stepmother of Abraham Lincoln

DENNIS AND JOHN HANKS
Cousins of Lincoln's mother

WILLIAM H. HERNDON
Law partner of Lincoln

DAVID DAVIS
Judge who rode the Circuit with
Lincoln

JOHN G. NICOLAY
Private secretary to Lincoln

JOHN HAY
Private secretary to Lincoln

JOSHUA F. SPEED
Lifelong friend of Lincoln

ORVILLE H. BROWNING
Senator from Illinois

NOAH BROOKS
News correspondent

HORACE GREELEY
Editor, *New York Tribune*

STEPHEN A. DOUGLAS
Senator from Illinois

ISAAC N. ARNOLD
Member of Congress

JOHN C. FRÉMONT
Explorer and soldier

MRS. JOHN C. FRÉMONT
(Jessie Benton)

WILLIAM SPRAGUE
Governor of Rhode Island and Senator

MRS. WILLIAM SPRAGUE
(Kate Chase)

ULYSSES S. GRANT
General

MRS. ULYSSES S. GRANT
(Julia Dent)

HENRY W. HALLECK
Major General

WILLIAM T. SHERMAN
General

DAVID HUNTER
Major General

CARL SCHURZ
Major General

GEORGE B. MC CLELLAN
Major General

ELMER E. ELLSWORTH
A protégé and favorite of Lincoln

HANNIBAL HAMLIN
Vice-President, Lincoln's first term

ANDREW JOHNSON
Vice-President, Lincoln's second term

MATHEW B. BRADY
Master photographer

WARD HILL LAMON
Law partner, companion, bodyguard

WILLIAM H. SEWARD
Secretary of State

SALMON P. CHASE
Secretary of the Treasury

WILLIAM P. FESSENDEN
Secretary of the Treasury

SIMON CAMERON
Secretary of War

EDWIN M. STANTON
Secretary of War

EDWARD BATES
Attorney General

JAMES SPEED
Attorney General

MONTGOMERY BLAIR
Postmaster General

WILLIAM DENNISON
Postmaster General

GIDEON WELLES
Secretary of the Navy

THOMAS CORWIN
Minister to Mexico

JOHN J. CRITTENDEN
Senator from Kentucky

HUGH MC CULLOCH
Secretary of the Treasury

JOHN D. ALLEY
Member of Congress

WENDELL PHILLIPS
Abolitionist, agitator

GEORGE A. MEADE
Major General

EDWARD EVERETT
Orator

CASSIUS M. CLAY
Major General, Minister to Russia

CHARLES SUMNER
Senator from Massachusetts

JOHN A. ANDREW
Governor of Massachusetts

ZACHARIAH CHANDLER
Senator from Michigan

ANDREW G. CURTIN
Governor of Pennsylvania

BENJAMIN F. WADE
Senator from Ohio

OWEN LOVEJOY
Member of Congress

GEORGE W. CURTIS
Editor, *Harper's Weekly*

NATHANIEL HAWTHORNE
Author

GEORGE BANCROFT
Historian

FRANCIS B. CARPENTER
Painter

WILLIAM LLOYD GARRISON
Abolitionist

CHARLES A. DANA
Assistant Secretary of War

HENRY J. RAYMOND
Editor, *New York Times*

EDWARD DICKINSON BAKER
Senator, Major General

ALEXANDER H. STEPHENS
Vice-President C.S.A.

THADDEUS STEVENS
Member of Congress

HENRY C. WHITNEY
Law partner, Paymaster U.S.A.

AMBROSE E. BURNSIDE
Major General

MATTHEW SIMPSON
Methodist Episcopal Bishop

PHINEAS D. GURLEY
Clergyman of the church Lincoln
attended

LYMAN TRUMBULL
Senator from Illinois

NORMAN B. JUDD
Lawyer, Minister to Germany

THURLOW WEED
Editor, publisher, politician

HENRY VILLARD
News correspondent

JOHN A. KASSON
Member of Congress

HENRY L. DAWES
Member of Congress

JOSEPH MEDILL
Editor

JOHN MURRAY FORBES
Merchant

IRVIN MC DOWELL
Major General

JOSEPH HOOKER
Major General

ROBERT H. NEWELL
(Orpheus C. Kerr) Humorist

DAVID Ŕ. LOCKE
(Petroleum V. Nasby) Humorist

CHARLES F. BROWNE
(Artemus Ward) Humorist

GENERAL AND MRS. TOM THUMB
Midget callers on Lincoln

ANNA E. DICKINSON
Lecturer

JULIA WARD HOWE
Song-writer

HARRIET BEECHER STOWE
Author

SARAH J. LIPPINCOTT
(Grace Greenwood) Author

ROBERT TODD LINCOLN
Eldest son of Abraham Lincoln

DAVID HOMER BATES
War telegrapher

HORACE PORTER
Brevet Brigadier General

THOMAS T. ECKERT
Chief of War Telegraph Office